HOW TO TALK TO YOUR CHILD SO THEY WILL LISTEN AND LEARN

Helping Your Child Grow into Success in Life

-Nick Gamis

reader. Under no circumstances will any legal responsibility or blame be held against the publisher for any reparation, damages, or monetary loss due to the information herein, either directly or indirectly.

Respective authors own all copyrights not held by the publisher.

The information herein is offered for informational purposes solely and is universal as so. The presentation of the information is without the contract or any type of guarantee assurance.

The trademarks that are used are without any consent, and the publication of the trademark is without permission or backing by the trademark owner. All trademarks and brands within this book are for clarifying purposes only and are owned by the owners themselves, not affiliated with this document.

Disclaimer

Please note the information contained within this document is for educational and entertainment purposes only. Every attempt has been made to provide accurate, up to date and reliable complete information. No warranties of any kind are expressed or implied. Readers acknowledge that the author is not engaging in the rendering of legal and financial, medical or professional advice. The content of this book has been derived from various sources. Please consult a licensed professional before attempting any techniques outlined in this book.

By reading this document, the reader agrees that under no circumstances are is the author responsible for any losses, direct or indirect, which are incurred as a result of the use of information contained within this document, including, but not limited to, - errors, omissions, or inaccuracies.

Table of Contents

Introduction

This book came into existence for a myriad of reasons. First, as a young mother, then as a nurse, and finally as a grandmother, I hope I have learned to be good at all the parenting skills necessary to raise happy, well-adjusted children, and people who actually contribute positively to the world. This may sound a bit jaded, and maybe it is. I apologize for sounding this way. It just seems the news is full today of people being evil to each other, I must wonder where it all begins. Does it all go back to our childhood? To our parents? To our society?

As we all know, children do not come into this world grasping and instruction book in one tiny hand, hopefully, written by the Almighty, to tell their parents how to be good at everything that is going to happen over the next twenty years or so of our children's life. It would be great if they did, but the greater power, in their infinite wisdom, left us to learn on our own. Parenting is not easy, and a lot of it is trial an error, to be sure.

My child was in kindergarten when I, myself decided to go back to nursing school. It was a promise I had made to myself for years, and I looked forward to it with great anticipation. Not only learning how to take care of sick people but to also learn how to take care of my child and my family. This included being all wise in the levels of child development, and how to be a pro at it. Sadly, I was mistaken.

Remember that while we did touch on what is supposed to be normal stages of growth and development of children, we were also charged with taking care of children. I mean, sick children. Sometimes, very sick children. That turns out to be another whole chapter in the theory of child development; or is it?

I don't remember exactly when the light switch was flipped, but I do remember realizing that children, either well or very ill, are just that—children. They need to be sometimes led to making the right decisions in this life. At least, what we consider to be the right decisions.

As my career progressed, I found myself in situations that all the nursing school training in the world could not have taught me. In the last few years, I specialized in correctional nursing. Sometimes, at the prison level, sometimes in the local goal. What I found there was amazing to my mind and was just downright bewildering.

Grown adults, who lacked the basic skills necessary to live in today's world. People who felt it was perfectly okay to take from others. People who were somehow stuck in some stage of child development that their psyche told them was a safe and just place to be.

It amazed me to think that as I grew older, my clients/patients became younger and younger. It was not uncommon to find people barely old enough to be adults behind prison walls, sometimes for a very long time. So, I started thinking. What went wrong?

Was it something in their early years? Dysfunctional family, perhaps? Poor parenting? Poor choices made? No one to turn to for help? Of course, I had no way of knowing, but I do feel that a lot of these young people were never taught to listen or learn. At least, judging them (which I try very hard not to do) by their current behavior.

Another thing that always amazed me was the varying levels of education these people had during their life. Some of them were indeed high school dropouts. Some of them didn't even make it to high school, for one reason or another. A few had college degrees. A very few had advanced degrees, yet here they all were behind bars for some reason or another.

I couldn't help but think that at some point in their life, someone let them down. Perhaps it was a parent. Maybe it was a teacher. Maybe it was someone else but had someone failed to communicate with this person. Yet, raising a child is such a complicated issue, it could be any number of things.

In my green years as a nurse in a correctional facility, I stumbled on a young man who was in custody for allegedly breaking into homes and stealing other people's stuff. It didn't matter to him if the family was home or not; but, to his credit (maybe that's the wrong word to use here), he never hurt anyone. He usually broke in during the day, hoping that the homeowner was out running errands or at work. He took what he stole and sold to people. It was how he made his living—such as it was.

He wasn't even out of his teens. He was pleasant, respectful and cooperative. He should have been worrying more about going to his senior prom, or buying his first car, or even if he were going to college; but no. He was behind bars. It was sad. I remember asking an officer with me about the kid. I asked about his family and his parents.

"I don't know about his mom," I remember the Cop saying. "But his dad is in the cell next door."

My circular thinking took me back to those early days of nursing school. Of early childhood development classes. Of what is supposed to be, and what isn't true in every single instance. That is what led to this work. It took many years for this work to come to fruition. It took a lot of studying, analyzing and life experiences for me to even begin to put words on a computer screen about this.

For years, I have been a student of the human mind. Specializing in mental health, I've had the opportunity to talk to many individuals who have made mistakes in life. I have met those who are sorry for the choices they made. I have also met many who blame others for their current station in life. I have worked people who have tried to fool me, patronize me, manipulate me, and outwit me.

Yet, I truly believe that it all begins at a very early age. It begins with an empty slate if you will. A child comes into the world with nothing but the autonomic system working and the five senses. It is the things they are exposed to over the years that make them what they are as an adult. So, am I saying it is nurture over nature? No. Not entirely, for I also know that people are born wired a little different than everyone else.

By that I mean they have mental and emotional issues that must be dealt with. These issues are not necessarily something that happens overnight. Coming from dysfunctional families certainly don't help; but, what if—what if—by talking to children so they understand respect for themselves and others is a good stepping stone? What if by talking to children so they will listen to builds upon or goes hand in hand with respect, and finally, what if we all talked to our children so they can learn, would it not be a good start?

If one parent gains any grain of knowledge from this my goal will have been met. If one child is not made to suffer from social bias, another will be checked off the list. So, please enjoy.

Section 1:

Respect

Chapter One:

First, there is Respect

Kids come screaming into the world as perfectly imperfect. Their tiny bodies are complete. Everything is working as it should. They cry when they are hungry. They cry when their bottom needs attention. They cry when they have tummy aches. They are born with an innate ability to let their parents know that they require something, but that is about all.

While I daresay that each child is born with the fundamentals of a personality, they are born with little other mental how too's on their list other than crying. I do not mean to imply that babies are mentally blank, for they definitely are not. Their little brains are going ninety miles an hour learning about the world around them.

They learn about that funny feeling in their tummy when it's empty. They learn when they are uncomfortable if they are too hot or too cold. The key thing is, they are learning. Over the months that follow, they are learning at an incredible rate. In fact, they are leaning so fast, if an adult had to learn at that mental capacity, our brains would likely explode.

Our world today is different than it was just one or two generations ago. There is so much out there on social media, YouTube and other electronic media, it is easy for children to get the wrong impression. By that, I mean they think that four-letter words, the F-bomb, bad attitudes, and lack of respect for themselves, their parent and their teachers is the social norm and it is okay for them to act in such a manner. I'm here, in my opinion, to say it is not.

We must teach our children to be respectful, and by that, I mean, from the day they are born until they are fully grown adults. Don't get me wrong. It sounds easy, but it is not. Today, many people want to be their child's friend—not their parent. I have witnessed many parents who do this and often even have the territory to act surprised when their child takes a wrong turn somewhere in this journey called life.

I truly understand that sometimes it's just plain easier to let a disrespectful action slide by. Parents are busy these days. Most parents have jobs, sometimes more than one, in an attempt to give their children everything, they never had as a child. They are just exhausted or too distracted by other things to respond to their kid's needs.

They do the best they can at the moment, then promise themselves they will do better the next time. What they don't get is that if they establish respect early on, there may not be a first time, much less a next time. The following sections contain useful tips for those harried parents—and children. Let's not forget the children, because they possibly suffer most of all in these situations.

I vividly remember working in a small, but very comprehensive hospital early on in my career. This hospital offered surgical services and had several fine surgeons in residence. However, there was one who, shall we say, felt well above everyone else? To say he was arrogant would be an understatement, to say the very least.

He also felt, or presented the persona, of owning the hospital—which he didn't; but administration tolerated his attitude because he was simply that good of a surgeon, and his patients normally had a good outcome. Not only was he an arrogant man, but he also let people know it in many different ways.

He demanded respect, which he grudgingly received; but, worse yet, he had little for anyone else. He talked to the nursing staff like we were stupid. His patients sometimes complained about his brusque and sometimes insensitive bedside manner. Perhaps what was even worse was that he often brought his children along when he did rounds.

To the best of my memory, he had four or five. Most of the time, it felt like a dozen. They showed no respect for the facility or patients since they found having desk chair races up and down the hall fun. They threatened staff by making demands for snacks and drinks, and when they didn't get them, they threatened to tell their father. We were, in effect, harried, overworked and nonpaid babysitters. Talk about lack of respect!

They were a mirror of their father in more ways than one. Lake of respect was evident, and we often wondered if all of the children would grow up to be adults, or if something horrible would happen to them because they pushed the wrong person's buttons. To be honest, I don't know because the surgeon eventually moved to a new hospital taking his bodacious horde with him. I lost track of him over time.

How sad is it to be remembered for the behavior your children showed toward others, and not in a good light? Yes, I remember the surgeon, but the main thing I remember was the lack of respect he was teaching his children. He was their role model and should have been teaching them by example rather than by just letting them run wild to 'express themselves'. No, they weren't letting their personalities bloom, they were just being manipulative and arrogant, which reflected the model they were taught.

Question for Discussion:

We all like to receive respect; yet, respect is something that has to earn, at least in some people's opinion. How can you earn respect from your child? What are some ways they can earn respect from you?

Chapter Two:

Learning is Like an Onion

Most educators propose that the act of learning is like the layers of an onion. If you start at the very core, that is the really the basic seed or 'set' of the vegetable. You can sort of compare that to a newborn child. It is what begins to grow. It has the basic genetic information needed for the plant to thrive.

As the onion grows, more layers are added. If we compare this to our child, they first learn to physically hold their head upright, then roll over, then sit upright unaided. As time progresses, they learn to walk, talk, and think. Layer upon layer.

The same is true of behavior. As a baby learns that crying when it's hungry will get food, it applies it to other things. As they grow, if they want a toy in a store, and for whatever reason are denied, they will go back to what worked for them in the past. They will cry, scream, or throw a tantrum for the entire world to see.

Many parents give in and buy the toy. I've seen it happen personally. Maybe acting out will get that toy purchased for them or maybe it won't. It depends on the adult's reaction; but by avoiding the temporary embarrassment of the behavior, they are simply avoiding what may turn into a bigger tantrum or even worse behavior, down the road.

Back to onion analogy, if the parent has the presence of mind to approach the behavior calmly, pull the child aside and tell them why they cannot have the toy, and the consequences of the behavior if they don't stop, another layer to onion has been added. The child has now learned that a screaming tantrum will not get them what they want. On the other hand, if the adult gives in and buys the toy, nothing has been learned and the misbehavior will likely be repeated.

Question for Discussion:

Knowing that learning occurs in layers, much like the onion analogy above, what can you do today to start the process of changing an unacceptable behavior in you or your child?

Chapter Three

Timing is Everything

Before we delve deeper into the important topic of timing, let's briefly look at something that is sometimes surprising to a lot of people. I know that when I was growing up, my parents did not think I was that special, or it seemed to me they didn't. I mean that they knew that I and my siblings were not perfect. We made mistakes. We slipped up.

Sometimes, depending on the severity of the misstep, the consequences could come crashing down almost instantly. Not that they didn't try to look at all missteps from all sides, they did; but they certainly did not take the view that many parents do today—that their children are totally blameless and therefore, perfect. Have you noticed this?

This can happen early on in a child's life. In fact, it can begin as soon as your child is old enough to crawl or toddle around. You can also implement the changes if your child is older, or even in the teenage years, but the best time to change the setting in your home is today! The older the child, the more difficult the changes may be to implement; but it still can be done.

It is your job to be the parent, not a friend. It's up to you to teach him how to function in the big wide world out there. Not only on how to make a living and other life skills, but other things as well. This includes teaching him or her how to behave respectfully to others, including you.

How do you know when your child is crossing that imaginary line between good behavior and unacceptable behavior? Well, ask yourself this simple question: Would I let a total stranger treat me like that? How about the next-door neighbor? If the answer is a resounding 'no', then your child should not get away with it either.

Like mentioned earlier, it is always a good idea to catch the inappropriate behavior early on. However, some people wait until the school-age years or older before they try to change a behavior that is disruptive and disrespectful, and already embedded deeply into the child's personality. A previously accepted behavior is difficult to change but not impossible.

If your child is about to go into those 'terrible teen' years, a parent should really think about their child's behavior. While there are some conditions, such as ADHD, one must first recognize the behavior, accept it as being inappropriate, and make plans to change it.

This includes the whole family having to make a change, sometimes a drastic one, but a change none the less. In this day, there are many single parent homes. Sometimes, these homes have one child, sometimes more; but the important thing is that the whole family become engaged in the plan to change.

If you have a spouse or partner, it is important that you act as a team when it comes to addressing the child's behavior. Often times you may see one parent pulling in one direction, while another goes the opposite way. This will not work when it comes to changing behavior. In fact, children are so smart and so good at manipulation, they can spot this potentially favorable situation a mile away and can use it to out-manipulate one parent over the other.

Keep in mind that children, from the day they are born, use manipulation to have their needs met. Remember the crying baby comparison? They cry when they are hungry. They get fed. They stop crying. Manipulation success! It can continue far longer and for far more disturbing behavior than you may realize.

So, **first step:** Talk to the significant another adult in the situation. I mean, really talk. Sit down in a calm environment, explain what is happening and enlist their help and support during what could out to be a stormy time in the family dynamics and relationships. Plan ahead, not just for the moment, but for the times when interactions with your child could be critical. Together, form a list of rules that you expect the child to follow. Make it clear what consequences will follow the disrespectful behavior. In other words, come up with a plan of action and stick to it.

Second Step: Teach your child some basic social interaction skills.

When I was growing up, I was always taught to answer adults with 'yes ma'am' or 'yes sir'. We don't see that often these days, but it's still important to teach your child some basic manners, likin saying 'please' and 'thank you'. It costs nothing to be polite, and it's not hard to do.

Plus being polite shows empathy toward other people. 'Excuse me' or 'thank you' acknowledges the other person's presence or feelings and teaches kids to respect others. Disrespect is just what you think it is, the opposite of respect, and tells other's you really don't care about them or their feelings.

By the same token, it is imperative that you respect your child first. Even when they disrespect you, you should show them what you expect them to do. Pulling your child aside and giving them a crystal-clear message is essential. Even though you may be upset, shouting and yelling at them is showing the behavior they should not repeat.

These are trying times to be sure, but they are also teachable moments. Make your expectations clear. Be firm. Don't forget to follow up through with consequences tailored to the behavior.

Third Step: Be realistic

I know. We all have high expectations when it comes to our children but there might be a time when you may have to leave the lofty heights of the soaring goals you expect. Take for instance a simple family meal at a restaurant. Before even leaving home, you should sit them down and explain what behavior you expect from them. This helps them to understand what you expect, gives them a sense of security, and will know the consequences beforehand so they will understand that actions do have consequences.

If they meet your expectations, give them credit or reward. If not, then follow through on the consequences you explained if they did not follow the rules. The ride home may not be too comfortable for anyone, but it will help to clarify what respect is and how you expect them to behave. This leads to the next step perfectly.

Fourth Step: Clarify the Limits When Things Are Calm.

When the child is acting out is not the perfect time to talk about limits or consequences. After everyone has calmed down, don't rehash the whole incident; but recap what happened and the situation as a whole. This would be a good time to get your child's side of the story and hear why things happened the way they did. It may be very difficult, but it is imperative that you stay as objective as possible. Perhaps use the technique of asking your child to see the episode like he was on TV or on Camera during the time. Ask him or her their opinion. Ask how they could have handled the situation better.

Fifth Step: It's not Personal.

The truth of the matter is, more than likely, whatever happened was your fault. Also, don't compare your child to another. Your job is to just deal with the behavior as objectively as possible.

Feeling out of control and scarred can cause parents to overreact. Overreaction leads to being too strict or rigid. When they 'under-react', they ignore the behavior, or blame it on a 'phase'. Both behaviors can be bad, and does nothing to correct the disrespected behavior, and will not help the child to change his thoughts or actions to a more positive response.

If you haven't intervened early in life your children, it is not too late. Even in the teen years, if your child is constantly showing disrespect, you can begin to step in and set those clearly defined limits. Experts state that children really do want limits and discipline, even if they yell and scream that they don't. The message you are trying to send is that they are loved, cared for and that you really want them to be a success and to be able to function in the big bad world. They may not thank you for it, but remember, it's not about being them being thankful to their best friend. It's about being a parent and doing the right thing.

Question for Discussion:

We have discussed the importance of timing when teaching children how to have respect for themselves and others. It is best that teaching respect begins early in a child's life. As soon they can say words, please and thank you, should be taught. But what if the child is older? How would you approach the problem of teaching a school-age child, or even a teenager, how to show respect to others?

Section 2:

How to Get Their Attention

Chapter One:

How to Get Children to Listen

I believe it is safe to say that the way we talk to our children has a great impact on their ability to listen to what we say. Along with respect, our continued attempts on teaching our kids how to act and behave, and the talk we use, fits right in.

There are generally three ways we talk to them. Notice I used the word talk, not communicate. Talking and communicating or two totally different things. Do you want your children to respond to you? Of course, you do, but do you become frustrated when they just give a look or roll their eyes in response? It could be in the way you are trying to communicate with them.

Communication Type: The Aggressor

These parents yell—sometimes a lot. They yell so loudly; the neighbors can hear it. If they are out in public, the people on the far side of the store probably heard it too. They may make ideal threats that they, and their children, know will not come to fruition. They use words as weapons, using words as an attack mechanism. They often repeat the same threats over and over again, maybe using different words, but the meanings are the same. They become louder the more frustrated they become because it seems that the children aren't responding. The kids may feel put down and usually respond by acting more, being scared, yelling back, or generally ignoring the parent altogether.

Communication Type: The Passive

These parent communicators are the soft-spoken opposite of the aggressor. They use words and tones, thinking they are being a good parent, but in reality, the kids are often using them as a doormat. When pushed to the proverbial end of their ropes, they morph into an aggressor type.

Again, they may yell and threaten, but their behavior and demands do little to change the behavior of the children in question. Idle threats never carried out re-enforces the behavior and doesn't do anything to change it.

Communication type: The Assertive

By far, this is the most effective way to deal with children whose behavior you want to change. These folks, while firm, are consistent and clear on what they expect from their kids. They are also positive, warm and confident. They also follow through when consequences are needed in response to behaviors, but it shows the children that their parents know what they are talking about and listen to them.

Here are some tips for getting children to really Listen to you. Keep in mind that children are different, just as adults are. One approach may work for some, but not all and vice-versa.

Question for Discussion:

Do you classify yourself as 'aggressive', 'passive' or 'assertive'? What steps can you take to change your behavior today that will ultimately change your child's responsive behavior?

Chapter Two

How to Get Their Attention

Call the child by name.

This may seem simple, and it is, but using their name helps to get their attention before you tell them what you want them to do, or how you want them to behave. If a child is otherwise distracted, like playing with dolls or watching a favorite film, they may not hear you. Like some adults, children can only focus on one thing at a time. Call their name again, if needed, and make sure they are looking at you before giving further instructions.

Use positive language.

Not many of like the words 'no' or 'don't' constantly hurled in our direction all the time. Kids don't either. If we say, for instance, "don't drop that vase", that thought and the image of the vase leaving their hands play through their mind and BANG! The vase crashes to the floor in a thousand pieces.

Why not trying to tell them what you WANT them to do like "Hold onto that vase! It's a very special Vase." Yes, this is a unique style of communication that many of us did not experience growing up. It does require some thought and practice, but it can be well worth it if that vase stays in one piece.

Do away with words that belittle or ridicule.

"Acting as a baby" comes readily to mind as does, name calling, and shaming. This type of behavior only makes the child feel worthless and affects their self-esteem. Yes, kids to have self-esteem and other adult traits you wouldn't think of. In an act of self-preservation, they may well stop trying to communicate with you if you use this type of language.

If you want a positive and confident child, use words that will encourage them to try hard and to keep trying until they succeed. Kids learn by imitating the people they admire and will deliver the same respect and praise to others as it is delivered to them. Use the words, like, happy, good job, and the like to praise your child for the correct behavior.

Get down to their level.

We're not talking mental level here, although that may help. But what you need to do is get down so that the two of you can look at each other in the eyes. Sitting at the table, or squatting down, when talking with them shows them you care and what they should do. Not only does it demonstrate good manners, but it also helps you to listen to each other. Use your child's name over and over if you have too until you get them to look at you. It is always important that they look at you when you are giving instructions. It is important too that you model the same behavior in return.

Use your volume appropriately.

We've all heard the yellers. You know, the kind of people that make you want to put earplugs in your ears. You normally stop listening after a while. It's the same for your kids. Trying to compete with a yelling child is fruitless. No one wins. Decide to talk only after everyone has calmed down. Think about it like this, if you constantly yell for little things, how are kids going to know when something is really urgent?

I can relate to this in my nursing career. Most of the time, we used conversational tones, but after you get to know a person you work with, and their tone suddenly changes, you know something is wrong somewhere. When you hear that certain tone, you drop what you are doing and run as fast as you can toward the direction the voice came from.

Yelling from another room is also a way to get ignored. Sterner action, such as actually walking into the room, will get their attention much faster. Plus, if the wait for a commercial to interrupt their favorite show on TV, they will notice you quicker than trying to talk over the favorite character. Your goal is to model respectful behavior, and walking into the room instead of bellowing from the kitchen shows respect.

Suggest options and alternatives. Use the either/or method. It is far easier for a child to get the idea they must do something before something else happens. This is particularly important when it comes to giving instructions. For instance:

> ➢ When you put your coat on, then you may go outside
> ➢ Which pair of shoes do you like, tennis shoes or boots?
> ➢ When you finish your homework, you can play your video game
> ➢ Which book would you like to read first, this or that?
> ➢ When you get ready for school, you may play with your toys until it's time to go.

Using words like when and which give the child a choice—albeit a limited one.

They are not being overwhelmed by too many decisions at once, plus they are not losing total control over the situation. It also lets them know something is going to happen, such as going to school and will set a time frame for the activity they wish to do.

Using the word 'if' leaves the door open to some speculation on the part of the child. If denotes only certain options and children fail to see that as a positive thing. When you can, allow the child to help you solve a problem. Take for instance a toy on the stairs, and you say 'don't leave your toy on the stairs', try the approach of, "Tom, think about where your toys go. Remember the time Dad stepped on your toy on the stairs and broke it? Where would be a good place to keep it so that won't happen again?"

Try to offer alternatives rather than saying a flat out "no" or "don't." For example, "You can't get the paints out just now, but you can draw with the crayons instead."

Keep it simple.

Too many directions given in a single setting is difficult for young children to follow. In other words, they are not good multi-taskers. Try to group requests into smaller bunches. Sometimes, it may be necessary to give a single direction, wait until that is done, and then state the next. While we want to improve our communication with our kids, be receptive to their level of interest in the conversation. If you are getting a blank stare, call it quits. If you feel as though you're rambling on, or talking above their level of understanding, try to use a more direct approach next time you visit the subject.

Question for Discussion:

Why is using words like 'when' and 'which' important when giving options to your child? Why is 'if' and open door that often leads to confusion?

Chapter Three

Nagging is a "No-No".

Keep away from nagging.

Nagging really doesn't work. Not for children. Not for adults. Most people tend to tune out the constant nagging about things, such as chores that need to be done, homework or other things we all face every day. Think of it this way—do you like to be nagged to complete a task that you know you have to do?

One way to keep this from happening is to make everyone responsible to keep up with their individual tasks that need to be completed. I for one do not keep a running inventory of every single replaceable item in the house. How many times have you gone to the refrigerator to get milk, and you discover the spot where the milk usually stays? Worse yet, how many times have you picked up the carton and find it empty except for a few drops? Aggravating, isn't it?

I resolved years ago that I would not become a 'nagger'. I would also not be responsible for going through the cabinets looking for things that we were running low on, so from the time my kids were old enough to understand if they saw we were about to go to zero on something, they were to tell me. As they got older, they could write it on a list. I've always kept a tablet and pen in the kitchen, so that anyone (these instructions included my husband), could conveniently jot down needed items.

If they were in a hurry, sit the container near the list and someone would write it down for them at some point. The whole goal of this exercise is that an item will be replaced, I will not have to nag at other people in the house, and there would be no name calling or finger pointing if something was missed.

Another easy solution to a problem, such as a child cleaning their room, taking out the trash or whatever chore needs to be done would be to create a job chart. Each person in the house would be listed on the chart along with the list of chores to be completed. Set a day of the week and make sure everyone knows what their assigned tasks are. You can rotate the jobs weekly or monthly so the list would change, avoiding people becoming bored with the same old tasks all the time.

Keep in mind that it is imperative that the whole family is included in this initiative from the very beginning. It would be helpful for all to sit down and agree on the type of chores and the terms of the agreement of the chart. Involving all the involved individuals makes it clear from the start what the chart is, the purpose of it, and everyone's expected participation. By having everyone work on the chart together, you are more likely to have more cooperation and more engagement than if the participants are suddenly thrust into the midst of a chart they don't understand.

The chart could list chores to be done on a daily basis or weekly or both. Young children love getting checks or stars added when the chores or done. It may also be helpful to set a time to do the chores. Maybe after supper, or when homework is done. The reward could be something very simple such as staying up half an hour longer or a special treat. The point is, it doesn't have to be elaborate or complicated. The rewards don't have to be either.

The point is, however, that everyone in the house knows what their tasks are, when they should be done, and the rewards or consequences depending on their efforts. Some child experts believe contracting with a child to do chores works well, and in a way, this is a contract geared more to the children's age.

It is necessary, however, to recognize your child's efforts and to give them praise and congratulations on a job well done. Rewarding the desired behaviors is especially important, as this will give the child a sense of accomplishments. Think of how you felt when your boss or significant other said kind words to you or praised your accomplishments. How did you feel? Happy? Pleased? Well, your child may feel the same when you tell them what a good job they've done.

Children do very well in a structured environment and when they know what is expected of them and when. Allowing for time for play along with time for homework and/or chores is a must. This will help to decrease those arguments and disputes between siblings and decrease the nagging going on in the house.

Also, remember that some children seek attention any way they can get it. This may include getting on your last nerve and refusing to do what they originally agreed to do. If this happens, don't resort to yelling or screaming. You are giving the child what was his goal—attention. While this is a good thing, do it the right way.

Stay calm and use the above tips to talk to your child. Point out that he/she agreed to the tasks and remind them of the consequences—again, what all agreed on—if they did not do the chores as agreed. Of course, you will have to hand out the consequences if they still do not comply; but it is important that you stick to your guns and don't go back on the agreement.

Model and expect good manners.

This is not an argument point or optional behavior on anyone's part. Remember that children learn by watching and are watching even when you don't think they are. The basic good manners of 'please' and 'thank you' should be incorporated early in their lives. They are not big words, and even toddlers who are just learning to talk can say them.

As a parent, it is our job to be a good role model, including good manners. It cannot be hit and miss either. No, you must be consistent so they will be too. Children are deserving of common courtesy too, just like the adults do. So, 'please', 'thank you', 'you're welcome' and 'excuse me', should be used even when talking to your children, just like you were speaking to another adult.

Be gentle but firm

As we discussed above, there are times when you will have to implement the consequences if your child has broken the rules or not done what was expected of them. Make sure that you and your significant other agree on the rules and stand as a team on this issue.

If one adult implements the correction and the other givens in, what is this telling the kids? Turning parents against each other is a favorite ploy, and nothing will be accomplished in a positive way if this happens. Of course, your child will not like it, but they know if the adults stand firm—and together—they will not even attempt playing one adult against the other.

Remember to use a firm tone when speaking of the requests. Make them sound like you mean it. Waffling in the breeze tells the child that you are not concerned and really don't care if you mean what you say or not.

Ask open-ended questions

As adults, we are pretty sure what 'yes' and 'no' means, right? Children do too and if you ask a child a question with a monosyllabic answer, that's what you'll get. In your mind, you may be wondering what your child is thinking, but asking the wrong type of question will not get you any closer to understanding the situation.

Try to ask questions in a way so that the child cannot simply answer with 'yes' or 'no'. This technique is known as 'open-ended' questions and will help to leave the door open for your child to explain what he/she is thinking.

Instead of asking, 'Did you have a good day at school today?', why not try asking, 'what new interesting thing did you learn at school today?'. I know that asking my daughter, 'did you have a good day at school today?' never got me very far. By changing the format in which we ask questions, we get more information and a deeper understanding of what goes on in our child's life when we aren't there.

Also, show your interest by asking, 'really?', 'What about...', 'I understand.', or even stating 'Wow, that's interesting!'. Don't fake it either. Children pick up on sincerity, in words and actions, and are really hard to fool. So, show real interest in what they think and feel.

Questions for Discussion:

1. How can nagging behavior be avoided at your house?

2. How do you think you will know if you are being too flexible or too rigid in your expectations when it comes to a job chart or other encouragement activity?

3. What are some special rewards you can think of that you can give a family member who has done a good job on something or changed their behavior to an acceptable form?

Chapter Four

Are you Getting Through?

Check for understanding

You talk and talk to your child and all you get back is an eye roll or a blank stare. Are they confused? Have they tuned you out, or do they simply not understand what you're saying? Are they confused by too many instructions at one time?

One way to check to see exactly what is going on is to ask them to repeat back to you what you have said so far. If they can't, you know that the conversation is either way too long, or way too complicated for them to understand. If this happens, stop and take a deep breath, then try to rephrase your question or words into shorter sentences. Try to be as clear as possible and use terms appropriate for the child's age and level of understanding.

Using "I" words is okay

While this may sound a bit odd, since it is the child's behavior or lack of understanding we are concentrating on, but it will work. Commands don't work all the time. Instead of saying, 'Sit down in the chair' for instance, try "I would like for you to sit in the chair, please."

This is kinder if you will, and softer approach. It also gives the child the same courtesy of good manners and also lets kids know how you feel about their behavior. This approach allows youngsters to think about how their actions are affecting you and other people around them. Using this technique, it also gives them the opportunity and obligation to change their behavior, if needed. Children really do want to please you, and by simply saying 'when you...I feel...because...' words, you give them a better understanding of how their actions affect you and why.

Give notice

None of us like to be broadsided out of the blue. It's like going through an intersection in your care and getting slammed into by a dump truck. The same can be said for your child who is busy playing or watching a favorite TV program and you suddenly grab them up and tell them it's time to go. You don't like being surprised this way, and neither does your child. So it is always a good idea to let the child know what is going to happen before it occurs. A few minutes before it's time to leave home for the store, tell them. For instance, "Tom, it's time to go to the store, so when this TV show goes off, get your coat, please."

Use inquiry-based listening

We have all seen the classic old TV shows where Dad is sitting at the breakfast table reading the newspaper. Mom is cooking breakfast, and one or two kids are sitting at the table, perhaps talking to each other about something that happened the day before or school in general.

In the old black and white shows, Dad is never too busy to put the paper away and join the conversation, perhaps delivering some lesson in his all-knowing way. Mom is also involved even though she is busy laying out a full continental breakfast for the family but manages to add her two bits worth of wisdom along the way. We all know that this really works in the make-believe TV land, but most mornings its total chaos trying to get out the door, handing each child a toaster pastry to eat in the car on the way to school.

The important thing to remember is if you don't have time to give your kids your full attention at that moment, don't pretend too. Tell them so and promise to make time when you can listen. Make an appointment with them for that evening or at your first free time and keep it. Clear your schedule for that time and sit down, face to face with the child.

Listen closely to what they are saying while making eye contact. Have them start at the beginning and verify to them that you hear them by restating the details back to them. Trying to say, 'how does this situation make you feel?", or "Do you mean...?". Making time for one on one conversation is really important. Your actions speak louder than words when it comes to showing your child that you really are interested in them and their feelings.

This can get a little dicey if the situation includes more than one child and if there is a considerable age gap between them. Older brothers or sisters sometimes talk over the younger ones, and sometimes the younger ones prefer it that way.

Sometimes older children talk above the heads of the others or talks about things the younger ones simply don't have a grasp of.

43

Older children often need more stimulating conversation and more information, so sometimes it is just plain easier to talk to each child individually, at their level and understanding.

Take the opportunities as they come when driving to the store, school, or anywhere else, working it into your day. This shows each child that you are listening to them individually. It makes them feel secure and they also know that you care when you take the time for them.

Don't sweat the small stuff

This is the title of a popular self-help book. The secondary title is 'and it's all small stuff'. This is essentially not true, especially when it comes to your kids. However, while trying to enforce your rules, it is an apt suggestion. Kids tune you out if you continuously lecture them over every little thing that you think is inappropriate or bad.

"Ought too..." often turns into a lecture in a child's mind, for instance. We usually tell children what they should or should not do, so they do not think for themselves sometimes. Here again, using an open-end question approach may help. Why not try, "What is it that you find so hard to understand?" maybe be better than "You must follow all instructions, or you'll mess up." If you are seeking a more connected conversation this is a good way to get it. The young one will have to think of a solution and a way to get there, whether it is a behavior issue or another problem. Your kids will likely listen better when you have to enforce a rule of a more serious nature if you let them work through their own solution.

Be considerate

Do you talk to your children like you speak with your friends? Is it with the same attitude, tone, manners, and courtesy? If not, maybe you should. Earlier we discussed that you are not your child's friend first. You're their parent, but in the day to day life, kids deserve the same consideration as other people in our lives. This way, you show your child that you love them and accept them, even though you are their parent. You love them unconditionally.

Kids too, need to know that you listen to them and this includes not interrupting them if they are trying to tell you something. If you do, just like your friends, they will stop trying to share their stories, their feelings or their lives with you.

Discussion Question:

Sometimes how you say something is more important than the actual content of the statement. What words can you use to make sure the conversation is understood?

Section 3:

How to Talk to Kids So They Can Learn

Chapter One

How emotions affect the brain

As adults, we can look back on our younger selves and think of things that scared the living daylights out of us. At that point and time in our lives perhaps we didn't have the developmental skills necessary to analyze and sort out what scared us so badly, so it was stored in our long-term memory as something so frightening and so traumatic, it scarred us for life.

You must remember that we, as human beings, have two types of memory. The first is short-term memory, which is classified as things that happen in the here and now. We can remember a question we were asked thirty seconds ago, as an example, and can hopefully answer it correctly.

Long term memory stores things that happen, but in a different way. Our brains take that short-term memory if it is traumatic or another event with life-impacting importance and stores it in the area of our gray matter designated to never forget what happened.

Like adults, children have both types of memory, but depending on their age and developmental status, their memories are more unstable, for lack of a better word. When children are scared, frustrated, in a state of despair, worried, sad, or shamed, children go into a kind of 'vapor lock' of their brain and lose the connection to their memories, ability to reason, and the ability to connect one event to another.

Kids freeze up sometimes. It is just in the way their brain is made. It is a sort of protection mechanism which is designed to keep them from being overloaded, overwhelmed or threatened. It is when a flood of emotions and other contributing factors threatens the child's well-being that this mechanism goes into full force to protect them from harm.

Having to take a final exam, for instance, is a complex action. It requires memory, reasoning powers, writing, planning and often organization of all of these. It can be enough to make some kids freeze up solid. It is no wonder that kids experience anxiety when their brains suddenly lock up like an engine who is out of oil.

The mere thought or sight of a printed page sliding across a desktop in their direction can make not only their brain shut down but increase the signs of flight or fight. Their bodies flood with adrenaline. Their heart rate goes up, their respirations spike, and every single body system goes on high alert.

When the brain goes blank and the rest of the body goes into autopilot, anxiety threatens to overwhelm. This means the child has basically shut down mentally, but emotionally and even physically, they are a mess. Unfortunately, in today's society and especially in classrooms, we see this happen frequently.

In these situations, the child doesn't do well on tests. Why should they? The mental facilities are negatively affected by all that bad energy. Flip the switch on for high emotions like these, and the switch for learning is turned off.

It has only been in the last few decades that objective data and studies from the field of neurology are backing up what scared, emotional, sensitive children have known for years. It has much more to do with the very basic systems of our brain that we ever thought before.

There is part of the brain called the Limbic System. Buried deep in the brain, many experts believe this is the part of the brain that kept our ancestors alive millennia ago when we first crawled or slithered from the primordial ooze. The is the part of the brain that controls a lot of our normal day to day functions, including learning, memory and our ability to make connections to other parts of the brain, including long-term and short-term memory.

Looking at the brain as if it were a holographic 3-D hologram, you would be able to see the brain from side to side, front to back, and from top to bottom. Imagine, if you will that your brain is like a multi-level shopping mall.

On one side, there is the left hemisphere. Here are the seats for logic, thinking in sequence, the concept of time and the words we speak. On the other side, known as the right hemisphere is where your body processes the knowledge of the space you occupy, guessing or intuition and the mathematical processes.

The frontal lobes of the brain are the place where most of our personality resides and also helps to coordinate the information from the back of the brain, where most learning, knowledge, and experiences are housed.

Finally, we move from the bottom of the brain to the top, sort of like an escalator. The brain stem, which actually sits atop the spinal cord and below the big part of the brain controls the automatic functions of the body, such as breathing, heart rate, and temperature control. The limbic system is on the next level, and its function is to take the emotional value of what we perceive with our senses, and ultimately decides if that information is good, bad, neither here nor there or deadly.

Its multi-tasks functions include interpreting that information and sending it all over the body, including the other parts of the brain. If the all-wise limbic system broadcasts a red alert, it shuts down. The escalator no longer carries signals to the top floor, and everything goes into lockdown mode. On the other hand, if the limbic systems give the green light, the escalator runs quickly and smoothly ending up on the top floor which contains the learning center, the imagination station, and creativity center. So, as you see the analog through, emotions are the fuel for the escalator, as electricity would be in the mall.

Discussion Question:

Taking tests, especially ones like mid-terms and finals, can cause children huge amounts of anxiety. How can you, as a parent, help reduce it? What things can you do the night, or even days, before the test to help your child feel less stress and anxiety?

Chapter Two

How to Reinforce Positive Emotional Habits

Parents may not realize the important role they play in the development of their child's emotional health and behaviors. The mental habits, if you will, forecast, block, or encourage the ability to learn well while in school, just as they establish the way a child interacts—satisfactorily or otherwise—with the outside world. Children whose life has been centered around good and positive interactions carry that with them into all learning situations including the classroom.

Following are six concepts that if implemented in your child's life which will help establish and strengthen those positive interactions every child needs to succeed both in life and the schoolroom.

✓ *Trigger motivation early:* Confidence is not something that every child is born with. It is a characteristic that must be sewn and grown to maturity. Break down new tasks and tests of ability into manageable blocks or chunks. Do not give too many instructions or tasks at once as this can overload the child and can lead to failure. Monitor their progress, support their efforts, praise their accomplishments, and let them go center stage with their efforts. Competence comes with the mastering of each task and gives the child the chance to build upon that experience.

51

✓ *Curiosity Doesn't Always Kill the Cat:* When you're curious, your child is likely to be too if you give them the opportunity to step out on their own with their ideas. Embrace their curiosity as your own and let them ask questions. Encourage them to find their own answers, and if they are wrong, gently guide them to the right destination. Use your own humor, imagination, and risk-taking as examples of how to change their own world.

✓ *Nurture growth, knowledge, talent, and power:* Your child might be a whiz with computers, or they may dance like a ballerina. Whatever their unique talent is, find it. Do whatever you can, including budgeting money, time, and mental efforts for those talents. Just as everyone has strengths, they have weaknesses too; but, don't spend too much time on them. Focus on what your child is good at.

✓ *Encourage connections to the outside world:* School is not the end all and be all of life. It is important to make outside connections as well and make sure that there is a balance between the two worlds. Use your kid's experiences in both places together so that they can function well in both instead of one or the other.

✓ *What Your Child Grow:* Each child should have his or her own journal of life. When they are old enough, ask them to keep a diary. Even young children, too young to use words, can paste pictures on a page. Keep track of how the child grows by measuring them on a wall or door frame. Put their name, date, and age along with it. At some designated point during the week, ask each child about something new they experienced that week. It doesn't have to be record-breaking.

It just must be unique for them. Include yourself in this activity. You never know what you'll learn about yourself.

✓ ***Accept Weaknesses, laugh with Absurdities, and Challenge the mundane:*** Tall order, isn't it? But, finding humor in your own mishaps also sets the example for your children to do the same. Helping them to organize opportunities for the development of any type of talent helps to reinforce good character. By building good emotional habits you can help your child meet the challenges of growing up with a sense of optimism that is necessary to live a life filled with competence and joy.

Discussion Question:

A relaxed atmosphere and a good sense of humor are two very important things in life. It is the same with your child. How can you foster these two emotional stabilizers in your child's life?

Chapter Three

Who's the Child Here?

As a young mother, I remember walking with my daughter, who was a toddler at the time, into a store. A friend of the family walked up and gushed about what a beautiful daughter I had. Before I could even voice my gratitude for the compliment, the friend leaned down into my child's face and began talking loudly in some foreign baby language either my daughter or me understood. In fact, my child looked at me as if to say, 'what did they say, mom?'. The friend then said something along the line that not all children learn to talk at the same time do they, before turning dismissively and left. It was as if the person thought we were somehow below the normal intelligence level or something.

I remember being borderline mad at the person, then teetering on the verge of laughter. My child fully understood me, but that was because I always made it a point to talk to her like an adult, not like some blithering idiot. In fact, I have made it a practice to talk to my children, my grandchildren—or any child for that matter, like an adult.

I am not talking about discussing Einstein's' theory of relativity, but I do believe that children can be spoken to in a language they can understand. It does include the way some people tend to over-pronounce words and change the pitch and tone of their voice, the way some people do. This can actually catch their attention, and they will listen to the speech patterns and syntax. In their future, this can aid them in getting the emotional content down pat.

But speaking in tongues to babies, using infant speech with older children, or just not talking to children at all is not a good thing. Children learn a lot about their language skills from the people around them before going off to school. We want to model what normal speech sounds like. We want to show them respect through conversations. Here are just a few reasons why we should talk to kids just like we do other adults (at their level, of course).

- ✓ *Kids Learn Language from Us:* Whenever we talk to a child it is an opportunity for us to teach them grammar, sentence structure, vocabulary and much, much more. We all don't have to hold degrees in the English Language to teach them this. We just have to talk to them, using everyday language instead of otherworldly gibberish. Even very young children can discern what is real and what is made up.

- ✓ *Kids Learn Social Norms from Us:* We all perhaps know a child who cannot carry on a normal conversation when they should be able too. Some children do have speech problems which have a physical cause, but often it is because they have been around people who talk 'down' to them all the time. When children see their role model switch from ordinary English to nonsensical words around other small children, they figure this is normal speech. In other words, use the opportunity to teach your children how to speak normally. Worse yet is the person who refuses to speak to children at all. Children learn this as well and go silent.

✓ *Nobody Likes to Be Patronized:* We've all probably, at one time or another, been patronized. Basically, this means another adult has spoken to you as if you were a baby or infant and you didn't like it, did you? Well, children don't like it any better than adults. We will not argue the point that children need to be monitored, guided and supervised; but that does not mean that we, as adults have the right to talk down and belittle them. Kids just know as much about the world as adults do. They don't have the experience with life situations that we do, but that does not mean that they are less intelligent or smart than we are. We do need to talk with children about the world and what's going on in it. We simply need to answer their questions, to the best of our ability, as if they were another adult.

✓ *It's Easier to Understand:* Toddlers who are learning to talk are bombarded with a huge amount of information in the form of sounds, visuals, and other sensory input. When learning to speak, they must also figure out the rules, what is normal for their language, and what words mean. If you throw in a lot of nonsensical sounds, it just confounds them even more. It's just more information they have to address. Why add to it?

✓ *Being a Parent has Enough Problems:* During an average day, parents are urinated on, have to face poopy diapers, wipe up puke, and clean spaghetti off the ceiling. We have to wipe snotty noses, keep fingers out of light sockets, and stop kids from eating anything they pick up off the floor. In other words, life with a small child is full of mishaps, missteps, and embarrassments. Why add making strange noises at our children be added to the list.

✓ *Kids Already Feel Small in a Big World:* Their smaller stature and less than graceful movements already make children feel out of place. They may want to participate in big people things, but they are always reminded they are too little, or it's dangerous, for them to do so. This is probably one reason for frequent fit throwing and tantrums. Frustration sets in and children react the only way they know how.

✓ *It Helps Them Develop Problem-Solving Skills:* No parent worth their salt likes to see their child get hurt. From a scraped knee to a serious tumble, we want to teach them how to avoid it the next time. How does talking nonsense to a child accomplish this? Rather, would it not make more sense to give the child a big hug and say something like, "Are you hurt? I saw when you fell and scraped your knee. That's why it's important to look where you walk." A clear language which clarifies what happened also helps them to make the mental link between what went wrong and what happened because of it. It also helps them to figure out how to prevent it from happening again and to aid in problem-solving.

✓ *It Helps a Child to Develop Emotional Language and Literacy:* When a child is having a difficult moment, talking to them like an adult helps them to pinpoint and understand their feelings. Validating their feelings helps them to learn what feelings are. Talking to them in a language they don't understand won't help them resolve the issue in their minds.

✓ *It Helps Them Practice Conversation:* It's amazing how much a very young child can understand what you are saying before they even have the words to say to you. I remember playing ball with my daughter when she was barely able to set up by herself. When I put out several toys in front of her and asked her for the ball, she would roll the designated item toward me, then clapped her hands in joy wanting me to roll it back. Young children and kids know a lot more than we give them credit for and are happy and proud to show off that they understand what you are saying.

✓ *It Just Makes Things Easier:* Your world is built around your child if you stop to think about it. You think about the child more than yourself. You are constantly looking for dangers that normally you wouldn't give a second thought. You build your schedule around your child. You sleep when they sleep and so on. So, why do we make it even more demanding by using a different language for them? Instead, talk to them like an adult. It just makes things easier on everyone.

Discussion Question:

Talking to children like adults helps them to develop many skills, such as language, body language, and syntax. Can you think of other life skills that speaking to your child can foster?

Chapter Four

School-Age Children are Special

When your child goes to school, it is a life changing experience for both you, as a parent, and your child. Children of the school-aged years are no longer focused on you and home life. Their world just got a lot bigger, and it happened the moment they stepped across the threshold to the schoolroom door.

Their behavior not only changes since they are now exposed to the behavior of other children, but they are now also more focused on their peers and their own agenda in life. The changes in behavior and communication can be so sudden it seemed to happen in a flash and in a way, it does. You may be thinking, 'who is this child? It's not the same one I left here this morning." Did I mention school was life changing? Well, it will certainly change the child.

Communication

As a child grows and develops, they begin to see the world in a way they have never seen it before. Things were either yes or no, but now the child can are exposed to more things in the big wide world and they can be reflective on some things. They start to look for why things happen and begin to ask more in-depth questions about them.

School-age children (from ages 6-11) can think ahead and plan. The often do so with a purpose or end goal in mind. Yet, they are still impulsive and desire driven. This façade, for that, is what it is, hides the deeper personality traits, and you may be surprised how loving, kind, and wise they are inside.

This age group rides a roller coaster of emotions. Sometimes they are dependent and clingy, while other times they are rebellious and resistant to doing what their parents want them to do. They can throw tantrums with the best of them, and then become insulted if they are treated like babies and patronized.

It is not uncommon for kids this age to become doubtful of their parents and to criticize their decisions. While questioning is normal, it seems to really bother parents sometimes that their sweet, loving and obedient children have turned into characters they don't even recognize. Many fail to realize that this is normal, and the child is just trying to learn how to think for themselves and decide how they feel about things.

Even the way children talk and communicate has been known to change due to the change in their surroundings. While young, most children use one style and stick with it no matter the situation, but school-age children sometimes develop new ways of speaking and acting based on what they see their friends at school do, or what they hear or see on TV.

Many parents become alarmed when their child, who once shared everything, now has shut down and closed the door in relationships with them. Parents tend to forget that home is now only part of the child's world, and he/she must include that into their life as well.

Finally, this age group starts to develop a broader look at the world and may include a more specialized and sophisticated sense of humor as a way to connect. They usually enjoy telling jokes—usually the same one over and over—and puns. They love playing interactive games and they can, for the first time, start to understand grown-up type media. Their analyzing skills are growing too, and they can better understand the rules of games and sports.

How Parent Should Communicate

Previously we took a look at the changes that can occur when your child goes to school. As noted, this is indeed a life-changing moment for all involved. It can be a confusing time for you as a parent, as you find yourself dealing with new situations and new issues associated with the roller coaster of emotions that are bound to explode, sometimes without any notice.

Remember that for children feelings are really big! Emotions take up a lot of space in a developing brain and your child is working hard to learn how to become accustomed to having them and dealing with them. Parents haven't necessarily done anything wrong if there are an occasional kicking and scream fit, or emotional meltdown. It's just what this age group does. It is important to remember that will normal, any extreme is not. You should worry if your kids are unhappy consistently, over the long term and if the tantrums are for manipulation purposes.

It's also normal for children to get angry. When kids get angry, they are usually very vocal about it. Parents, being frustrated and not knowing what to do, yell back. Circular actions start and one thing leads to another, only escalating the episode to bigger and bigger fights, disagreements and tears.

But, what can a parent do? First, take a few deep breaths. Calm down and remember that all children, particularly this age, will have tantrums sometimes, and probably in the most inappropriate place possible. Try not to feel embarrassed by it. Parents everywhere are wondering how to deal with it too.

Often, tantrums are a means for a child to get their parents attention. Perhaps they feel as if they are being ignored. When you do stop to listen, try to accept the child's feelings, even if you feel they are ridiculous. Children who are learning often confuse actions and reactions. When things calm down, it is a good strategy to sit one on one with the child and delve into what happened.

It is also important that you validate your child's feelings and accept them. Use words that all involved can understand. Build a conscious awareness of the emotions involved and come to a common solution that is acceptable to everyone. But how?

Instead of Accusing, try describing the problem. When you do, instead of giving orders, kids are more likely to behave in a positive manner. Avoid shaming and pointing fingers at the child.

Give information, but don't accuse, blame or put down the child. Children again are more likely to change their behavior.

Give them a choice. Threats and commands make a child feel helpless. When they feel helpless, they are more than likely to defy your authority or defend themselves in other ways.

Using words or gestures that are short and to the point can also get your point across. Children of this age group do not have the attention span or short-term memory capacity to listen to long explanations or lectures. A single word or gesture communicates to the child that there is a problem and that they should start working out what needs to be done.

Describe how you feel in terms that do not demean or belittle the child or their character. Making it about the actions rather than the child will have a positive impact on the behavior.

Write it down if the talk is causing a shut down in communication on either side. It can be a simple note, humorous, a poem or anything that will trigger the child's thought processes and encourage the desired response.

Discussion Question:

Accepting your child's feelings is important to them and you. How does accepting and understanding emotions play a big part in teaching them respect, how to listen and how to learn?

Chapter Five

Self-Discipline

Is there such a thing as a child having self-discipline? Believe it or not, there is. According to the experts, when you're a parent and are thinking about discipline tactics, you should look at not like a way to control your child, but a way to teach your child how to control themselves. I know, that's something to wrap your mind around. But think about it like this, kids who learn self-discipline are better equipped to face life, its challenges, have good stress management and make healthy choices even when the parents aren't there.

There is s difference between being a well-behaved child and a self-disciplined child. Most children of school age seek immediate gratification of some need. A well-behaved child may ask politely before demanding that need is met. A self-disciplined child can do without that self-gratification need being met all together. They, in other words, make a good choice in behavior regardless of how they feel or what they want.

Take the scenario of going into a store's toy section with your child. They see a toy they want. You say no. While the well-behaved child may initially whine and cry, because they want that toy now, and you again explain why they cannot have it, they may be pushed past their threshold and a kicking screaming tantrum may follow.

The self-disciplined child on the other hand, and in the same situation, will be able to cope with the emotions and understands why they cannot have the toy. While they too may be upset, they do not impulsively throw themselves on the floor and kick and scream.

Self-discipline kids have also learned how to make healthy choices by looking at the positive and negative side of the issue. They recognize the importance of good decisions in terms of work at home and school, classmate pressure and how to take care of themselves.

The parents, unfortunately, are the ones who often take the blame for their child's behavior if self-discipline is not present. This often results in the negative behaviors of nagging, threats, and other self-defeating mechanisms. The more this behavior occurs, the less the child completes, and the parent ends up just doing the chores themselves.

One of, if not the most important task for a child to learn in early childhood is to develop self-discipline. Those who never learn tend to struggle with things through life like, how to keep healthy habits, managing chores and work, managing money and all other responsibilities all require this trait. But how do you teach your child?

Seven Ways to Teach Self-Discipline

1. Teach them to come to you when you call their name. While this may sound like something you would want to train your puppy to do, it is also important that your child learn this as

well. If the child is another part of the house, and you call their name, they need to physically respond and not just yell "WHAT?". Having eye to eye contact with your child is vital if talking about something. It is also important because it teaches a child that we must sometimes stop or give up something we enjoy in order to do something else.

2. Teach them to respond positively to correction. Who likes to be corrected? Even as adults it can be a hard pill to swallow sometimes, but children should be taught that negative reactions such as anger or a having a bad attitude are not acceptable. It is a valuable lesson to learn that we all are corrected at some point. A good attitude as well as appropriate behavior is hard to learn but one that is vital for success in life.

3. Social skills require self-discipline and self-control. Give your child praise and a pat on the back when they interact correctly with others. Not interrupting, anger control, keeping your hands to yourself, and reporting back when you have finished a chore all require self-discipline and control.

4. Encourage them to take on a sports activity, music lessons, a part-time job, caring for pets, or special learning activities. These can help build social contacts and self-discipline.

5. External rewards like payment for mowing the neighbor's lawn, checking off chores on a to-do list, are also a good opportunity to explain and implement self-discipline. Don't be preachy because this can actually backfire but let them know you are proud of their accomplishments.

6. Use everyday activities, such as bedtimes, to teach the concept. Some children and their bedtime routines turn into

a battle of wills between parent and child. It does take a lot of control for a child to stay in bed, particularly whenever everyone else in the household is up and doing fun things. It is important to create a routine for the child, such as brushing of teeth, reading a story, and other activities that signal it is time to sleep.

7. Morning routines can be just as challenging with chores and schedules. Privileges are a good way to underscore the importance of getting things done on time. Simple things of living are seen as the rewards of being responsible.

Some parent's goal is to give their children an easier way of life than they had. Other's vow to give them things but do so at the cost of responsibility and pay in ways they never would have imagined.

Discussion Question:

Do you think self-discipline if a viable option when teaching children how to become responsible adults?

Chapter Six

Crime and Punishment

There was a time in our country when parents lived by the adage, 'spare the rod and spoil the child'. Thankfully, this type of corporal punishment is used very little these days, according to some. There are many laws today to protect individuals from unfair and hurtful treatment. So what is would one consider corporal punishment of children?

Gershoff and Bitensky state that corporal punishment is 'The use of physical force, no matter how light, with the intention of causing the child to experience bodily pain so as to correct or punish the child's behavior'. According to this definition, that includes spanking, slapping a hand, face or another body part.

No one ever said raising children was easy. There are many challenges and one of the biggest is discipline. At times, it is difficult to balance the severity of the punishment with compassion. Corporal punishment, which posits that behavior will change because physical pain is applied therefore to those actions, can have a far more reaching effect than first thought.

Aggression

According to one study, children who were spanked were more likely to rationalize domestic abuse. Another study found a link between spanking and violent means of problems solving that went from the time they were victims until adulthood. There was also a connection between spanking and aggressive behavior, delinquency, and violent adults.

Mental Health

A negative impact on the mental and emotional health of children may occur. This happens when the emotions and guilt manifests in problems such as anxiety and depression sometimes years down the road.

Cognitive Impact

Corporal punishment may also negatively affect a child's cognitive development. Verbal, rather than physical, punishment has been shown to be more cognitively stimulating. One study revealed a correlation between academic performance and corporal punishment, wherein children who were punished physically were less likely to perform well in school and more likely to have classroom disciplinary problems.

Parent-Child Relationship

Children's relationships with their parents may be damaged by corporal punishment. Such punishment may encourage mistrust and hostility toward parents, effectively damaging other aspects of the parent-child relationship and breaking the bond of trust and love on which, all such relationships are based.

Discussion Question:

Do you think that corporal punishment on any level is acceptable?

Chapter Seven

Alternatives to Punishment

This is a very debatable topic in today's society. Some people do not like the term 'punishment' as it tends to conjure up ideas of bad, unfavorable, uncomfortable things. Some would rather use the word 'discipline', which basically means to teach. That's what parents do, every minute of every day, either by setting a good role model or setting and enforcing limits. But the question remains, how do you correct unacceptable behavior.

Of course, it has to be tailored to the age and abilities of your child. But here are twelve alternatives to punishment that will help you address choices and problems with the intent of forming an maintaining a positive, respectful and peaceful connection with your child. These are geared for the one to six years of age range.

- ✓ Take a break with your child. If you feel things spiraling out of control, and your child is making some bad choices, find a quiet place and sit together. Listen to what your child is saying and feeling. Just five minutes can change the whole day.

- ✓ Give a do-over. Also known as a second chance, explain why the behavior was unacceptable and give them another try to change the behavior.

✓ Solve the problem together. If you and your child are both feeling frustrated, allow them to take about the problem and then together figure out how to solve the issue.

✓ Ask questions when you don't understand why the child is doing—or not doing—what you asked. Listen intently and understand, then correct them by making the appropriate suggestion for resolution

✓ Read together. Find a story where the character messes up and how they made a better choice. Explain what the story is about and ask how your child can do the same.

✓ Use dolls, puppets or other toys to bring the behavior to a better understanding. You can also use them to make a resolution to the problem.

✓ Offer a choice of options. Make them safe, respectable and also acceptable. This helps with setting boundaries.

✓ Take a break and listen to music or a song to connect with your child and loosen the tension.

✓ Go outside or to another location to help redirect behavior to another direction.

✓ Breathe. Both parent and child can benefit from taking a few deep calming breaths before settling in to calmly discuss the issue.

✓ Find a chill-out or time-space that helps everyone calm down. A quiet place to think, a few toys to keep them occupied, and time to calm down before talking or being with others.

As with everything in life, every situation is different. So is every child. The above suggestions are certainly not one size fits all. You must customize the approach you use so that you and your young child are comfortable with them. Proactive tools like these are certainly better than waiting until the unacceptable behavior, which can be worse than something as simple as sharing a toy, surfaces.

Here are some alternatives for older school-age children. Some experts believe that they will work both at home and at school. Consistency, as we know is as important as the actions themselves.

Scenario: Your school-aged child is cursing loudly about having to do his chores.

Adult response: "I have told you and told you not use that type of language in this house. Now you're going to be punished!"

Instead why not try:
- ✓ *Step 1.* Make a point of a way to be helpful
  "I can hear the frustration in your voice. It would help both of us if you could express it without using foul language."

- ✓ *Step 2.* Verbalize your disapproval without attacking the child's character
  "That language upsets me and I don't like hearing it here."

✓ *Step 3.* State your expectations from the child
"I expect you to find some other means to tell me how upset you are."

✓ *Step 4.* Make amends (guide the child to show how)
"What I'd like to see and expect is a loss of some strong words that express your feeling rather than the ones I just heard. You can look them up on the laptop or use a dictionary."

✓ *Step 5.* Offer a choice of action
"You can feel free to curse to yourself—silently—or you can use different words that are not offensive."

✓ *Step 6.* Let your child experience the consequences (if he/she continues to do the behavior)
"When you continue to use those words, I lose the desire to help you."

Remember that you are the adult in the situation. You may have to give yourself some quiet time beforehand when it comes to addressing recurring behavior. If you lose your temper, it profits now one.

Let's take a moment to look at problem-solving. As in the scenario above, the final step could have the desired effect, or it may not. Let's take this one step further and involve the mother and son a step further in the problem-solving process. After finding a quiet place, sit with the child and ask him why he is so upset about having to do his chores. Note that we are not focusing on the foul language issue at this time.

✓ Listen to your child's problems and needs.

"I hate doing chores. All my other friends don't have the stuff to do and are out playing ball, and I'm stuck here doing homework and cleaning my room.

✓ Summarize what you hear your child saying as their point of view.

So you're telling me that when you here doing your chores
1. Your friends are outside playing
2. Your friends don't have chores and homework

✓ Summarize your feelings and needs
1. I understand that you feel that you are being treated unfairly.
2. We did agree together on these chores were to be done weekly, and your homework every evening

✓ Ask your child to help come up with some ideas to find a solution, write them all down—without commenting or evaluating
1. I shouldn't have to do chores
2. Homework could be done later in the evening, not when I get home
3. I could trade chores with sister because her list is shorter
4. I could do all my chores one day a week

✓ Decide together which ideas work, which you do, and how to put them into play
1. Everyone in the house has chores to do (agree)

2. Homework will go undone if you move it later in the evening. (Child reluctantly agrees). Also, the later you start homework, the later it will be when you are done and that means less sleep. So, break up your homework into chunks, do the easy part when you get home and the hard part later.

3. Sister's list is shorter because she is younger, and she cannot do the chores that you do, including cleaning your room.

4. Okay, we can look at the chore lists and maybe move some chores around, or you can move most of them to once a week.

The resolution worked well in this case. The negotiation process explained why things were the way they were. However, they were able to reach a peaceful resolution by moving things around on the chore board to allow more time to socialize and play ball with friends.

It is important to take the time to get a piece of paper and a pencil to write down the items in the process. Sometimes going the verbal route works, but there is a sense of interest on the part of the adult, and of permanence when things are in print. Seeing words will give visual cues of the child's thought process and may inspire him/her to continue this concrete way of problem-solving for years to come.

Discussion Question:

Often, coming to a suitable conclusion for all people involved in conflict takes the skills of an accomplished negotiator. What are some of the skills needed when negotiating with a child to find a better outcome for unacceptable behavior?

Chapter Eight

Praise without Demeaning, Criticism that Doesn't Cut

We are all tempted, at the end of a long day, to skip over some steps in teaching our kids how to be respectful, how to listen, and how to learn. After all, you have probably had to deal with grown up all day long. Grown-ups that perhaps weren't taught the basics when they were little, and you felt trapped and frustrated. You are tired, so you fall back into old habits because, let's just face it, that is easier than doing the right things.

But, perhaps that's a good time too. Maybe it's a good time to take a deep breath, have a minute of me time and to regroup before tackling the trial of the day, which could be your kids doing homework and chores while you are busy doing the laundry, cooking supper, and ten thousand other things all at once.

Let's face it. Kids are smart. They instinctively know when you are vulnerable. When you are distracted by other activities, or when you are multitasking, their radar dish starts whirling around and around and they know exactly the right buttons to push at the exact right time to make you want to blow your top! Right?

Why not make it a rule—even for yourself alone—that you take ten to fifteen minutes when you get home, find a quiet place, close the door, and decompress. It will save you a lot of frustration, your kids more than a few attention-seeking tantrums, and hurt feelings all around.

Once you have chilled out for a few minutes, you will feel more like attacking the next task, and the next, and the next, with—well, not exactly a renewed sense of purpose—but with a better balance of emotions and purpose.

So, let's look at a few ways that you can give praise with coupling that demeaning, sarcastic thought and also point out what is wrong without cutting criticism.

Scenario one: Bedtime without the hassle.

Pointing out What's Wrong is Wrong!

Mom: "How many times do I have to tell you to get ready for bed? You haven't brushed your teeth! Those PJ's have peanut butter all down the front! Bedtime is in 15 minutes!"

Childs Reaction: "I can never do anything right, evening getting ready to go to bed!"

Instead: Describe What the Child Has Done Right and What is Still to Be Done!

Mom: "Oh, look at you! You've already got your PJ's on! All that's left is to brush your teeth and you're ready for your story time!"

Child's Reaction: "I'll go do it now! Can we read a Clifford Story?"

Homework Trials:

Instead of pointing out what homework hasn't been done like:
Mom: "You've been sitting there playing! You haven't even touched those last three Math problems! If you don't hurry, it will be bedtime before you're finished!"

Child's Reaction: "This is hopeless. I'm hopeless."

Solution: Describe in a non-accusatory manner what they have accomplished and what is left to be done.

Mom: "Wow! You're almost done! You've already completed 3 math problems and you only have three left! I'm impressed!"

Child's reaction: "Wow, I can do this! I'm over halfway done!"

Sounds very simple, doesn't it? All you have to do is change just a few words and get your child into the moment while encouraging them to keep going. Remember, it is also about the unspoken message you are sending at the same time your saying the words. It's about body language, the tone of voice, and the quality of your words and actions combined.

It's important to also remember to:

1. Describe what you hear or see rather than evaluating
2. Describe what you feel
3. Point out what is left to be done, rather than criticizing what they have done.

We all have friends that can go a bit overboard sometimes. Some kids complain that their parents praise them too much! Is there such a thing?

Believe it or not, yes. A lot of children feel uncomfortable when parents are constantly mentioning their behavior, whether that behavior is good or bad. They feel like they are constantly being a watch, which they are. Some children get so used to the constant praise and feel lost without it and may even lose the confidence they once had in themselves because of it.

Then there is another group of kids who appreciate the praise but in a different way. Constant praise is a means to an end for these kids. They see praise as a form of trust from their parents that they are doing the right thing and will continue to behave as they feel appreciated.

There are also times when praise can be used as a directive to finish a task. Take for instance your child is working on a project for the science fair. They ask you how it looks. They may grumpily say that it looks awful, or not right, even if they are not finished yet. You are forced to decide between the approval of teachers, for example, or getting the child back on track. In this case, it is always best to choose the task over approval.

Comment on the project, pointing out how hard the child has worked so far, the positive points of the project, and how proud you are of them for finishing the project, even though they haven't yet finished it. The best and most enriching type of learning takes place when the child is involved in what they are doing, not what others will think of them.

Of course, approving of your child's behavior or hard work is good, but it won't last as long if the motives and feelings behind them aren't ingrained into a child's thought pattern. A good way to start is to describe an action before praising so that the child understands the emotion behind it.

Look at these possible descriptions.

"You knew I would be worried if you didn't get home at the time you usually do. Thank you for sending a text explaining that football practice ran over time. That's being considerate, and I appreciate it."

"Thank you for trusting me enough to tell me about the dent in the car bumper, even though you knew I might get upset. I appreciate you coming forward and being honest about it."

"What a creation! You made this science project out of paper and string!"

In the above cases, while you point out the instance when the child was considerate, honest or creative, there is no pressure placed on them to continue these behaviors, but with the right words and actions, they may well do so.

Remember, it is important that you should not push your feelings, interest, or habits on your children. It turns out that when you do, you are comparing them to you and are trying to pressure them into your way of thinking and/or behaving. It is a form of evaluating and can come across that way to a child.

Now would be a good time to address the issue of multiple children in the household. As we all know, each child is different in the family, just as there are different children in any group. You may have one child that does very well in school, while you have another who seems to struggle to get just mediocre grades.

It is so tempting to pour praise like sacred oil upon the head of the anointed one. But what about the other one who works just as hard—or harder—and doesn't do as well as his/her older or younger sibling? Will there be some resentment if you constantly praise the high achiever and ignore the other hard-working child? Of course, there's the chance of it.

It would be best if you took the opportunity when it arose to praise and show your appreciation to both siblings at the same time. When you're really impressed and pleased by something the achiever has done, you can describe it nonchalantly if both children are present. When you have the chance to have a private moment with the achiever, which is the time to tell them how impressed you are with their accomplishments, not when the other child is present. This way, you are less likely to cause a feeling of resentment between the two.

Many people think they are inspiring the underachiever when they brag on the other child in their presence. This couldn't be further from the truth. Often, comparing children leads to jealousy and bad feelings. Why do this to a child?

How to say, 'you're wrong' without saying 'you're wrong'.

As teachers, it is the parent's responsibility to be quick on the draw when it comes to validating a child's efforts. But, what do you do when your child asks you a query that tells you they are totally off the mark? At some point, you will have to address the issue, but how do you give them the right answer without making them feel hopeless?

This can be like walking a tightrope, in the dark, with no safety net below us to catch us when we fall. How much is enough information, how much is too much, and how much is too little? It is indeed a slippery slope, for each child is different. You must tailor your response to the specific child, in the current situation, at the right time. It sounds nearly impossible, doesn't it?

Well, think about it like this. As a parent, our role is not to supply all the answers to all the questions a child asks. Sure, there are sometimes when we have to answer questions or change the tack the child's thought process is taking, but that does not necessarily mean we give them the right answers all the time.

No, one of our jobs is to help the kid to come to the right answer or conclusion by using their own thinking and cognitive skills. It is almost like taking a child on a hike. The beginning of the journey is with the question or problem and guiding them in the right direction to reach the top of the peak of the high mountain of learning.

We begin by asking a child what made them want to know something. It should be done in a respectful way which will help the child form their own thoughts in a coherent manner, so they can put it into words. Sometimes they may trip over an obstacle that you, or they, may not see; but it is important to remember that the journey is half the fun.

Learning is fun if the child is enjoying the learning experience. You can actually watch a child when the light comes on and a spark of knowledge ignites. These children will actually bloom in front of your eyes if they are truly interested in the subject, and will dive into it like an Olympian in a swing pool given the right push.

Using the hike up the mountain analogy further, sometimes on a trail, you take a wrong turn. It is important that you stop, reconnoiter and backtrack if the need be. Once you reach the main trail again, keep going until you find your way to the top, or in this case, the right answer.

Discussion Question:

How do you tell a child 'you're wrong' without saying those words?

Don't Typecast Children

Another point to remember is that our words are sometimes like telegrams which tell children who are what they are. In effect, we must avoid the opinions of other people, who knowingly or not, label children with names like 'forgetful', or 'lazy'. That is why we must also be so careful when we label children with disorders like attention deficit disorder, or other mental and emotional problems so that we don't pigeon hole them into a life that isn't lived to the fullest because of their diagnosed disabilities and shortcomings.

Subconsciously, we are prone to categorize these kids into their disorder descriptions. We are only human, after all, and that is just how our brains work, trying to make sense of the situation. We find ourselves making excuses or not really trying to learn how we, as adults, should help these children learn and not just put them on a list of someone else's making.

Keep in mind that these children deserve the same respect we demand. This takes some planning and thought, but it is necessary if we are going to teach children how to respect, how to listen and how to learn.

Your plan should include the following elements starting with looking for every opportunity presented to us to show the child a different, new picture of themselves. You probably have been labeled in your life at some point, right?

Maybe your significant other called you lazy when they came home from work and the house was a mess. No matter what you spent the day chasing two toddlers' around and trying to work a part-time business too. That label of 'lazy' made you feel unappreciated, perhaps. Maybe even make you angry, but when you hear that word applied to you day after day, you come to accept it as truth. How did it make you feel? Miserable? Hurt?

Well, children feel the same way and often will become the thing they are being labeled, even if they are not in the beginning. They feel hopeless and helpless and eventually to avoid feeling that way, they accept what they are being told as truth.

The next step in your master plan should be to include the children in situations where they can see themselves differently from the label, they have had stuck on them. Give them a chance to see that they are not lazy, for instance. Or, that they are not forgetful. Honest praise is necessary for this step. Real, honest praise for completing a project that was a lot of work, or praise for remembering to gather their coat, gloves, and backpack—without having to be reminded—for school.

In the next part of the plan, remember to say something positive about the child to a friend, partner, or someone else. I know that eavesdropping is considered impolite, but in this case, when a child overhears you telling others about their good behavior or good actions, it's okay. Knowing that you are proud enough of their efforts to talk to other people about their accomplishments when they don't think they are listening will give a much-needed boost to their self-esteem.

Step four includes remind your child of the past successful endeavors. They are not failures at all things. As long as they keep trying, they will succeed. Seeing oneself as failure leads to more failures. Seeing you as success leads to more success.

Finally, it is vitally important to let the child know your feelings and expectations. How are they really supposed to know what is expected unless you tell them? They are not minding readers, after all, and they may think that you want one thing when the truth is in the opposite direction. This works well with almost any age child and can be modified by changing the words to the right age level.

By changing yourself first, you can change the way your child acts and behaves. Every child, just like every adult, has different characteristics in different settings. What you see at home may not be applicable to the child when they are at school, out with friends, or in any other number of situations.

Until now, we have been talking mainly about 'Bad labels' we paste onto children's personalities; but, what about the opposite end of the spectrum? The exceptional children, the artistic children, and the child prodigies out there that gains our attention by being outstanding in music, sports or the arts?

No more signaling them out either. They do need support and praise as well, but don't they all? Every kid needs to be encouraged to experience life, including sports, arts, and/or music. Not every child can be the star quarterback, nor should we expect them to be, but those that are blessed with talent should not be labeled any more than any other child.

One trap we, as parents, often fall into is telling a child they are 'always' something. Always late. Always dirty or messy. Always forgetting things. This may not seem to be a label, but it is. By telling a child they are always something, puts them in a corner that they find they can't get out of. They will do one of two things: They will continue to be late, proving you correct; or, they can change their behavior to the opposite to prove you wrong. Instead, tell them that they choose to be the way they are and find a way to help them change the behavior if needed.

The same can be said of those children we label as 'always good', or always special, or always academically gifted. Let us stop and realize that even labeling with good things can lead to the same problems.

Let's say little Sally is always academically gifted. Let's also say that—heaven forbid!—little Sally fails at something. Perhaps that is too much. Maybe her grades drop. She's been sick. Or perhaps it's just a course that she's not interested in. What happens then?

She suddenly finds herself crushed. She's always good academically anymore. She has pride in the fact that she breezes through her subjects, or had until that point, and now what? Suddenly she feels worthless and hopeless. It doesn't matter that she had six other 'A' grades on that report card. All that matter is that one grade is not good.

So, are you guilty of labeling your kids? Are you the one who is labeling them with names or attributes that are somehow holding them back? Well, that's certainly something to think about, isn't it?

Discussion Question:

One should never typecast a child. What words do you use that can make that happen?

Conclusion

Wow, we have covered a lot of information on these pages. We first began our journey together by learning about respect. We started here because it is a fundamental building block when it comes to children learning about how to respect themselves, their siblings, their peers, their parents and anyone else they may meet during their lifetimes.

Learning is something the onion analogy we used early on, or perhaps like layers in a cake. One learning experience leads to an understanding of a principle, which is then added too by the next experience and the next and so on.

It is important to point out at this time that people should learn their entire life, not just the time they are in school or college. When one stops learning, no matter their age or vocation, they cease to push the boundaries of the environment. The become stagnant. Eventually, they can become biased, bigoted and closed-minded, so yes—learning respect is but the first step in a long process of learning new things, new ideas and new inventions.

As children, we are a clean slate. We come into the world knowing nothing except to cry when we need our needs met. While this is a good communication tool when we are infants, it doesn't work so well as we get older, but there are some people who never learn this important lesson. They become stuck and fall back on the ways that granted them success in the beginning.

As a nurse in corrections, I was fascinated by the inmates I worked with on a daily basis. Some of them were master manipulators, using whatever means at their disposal to obtain whatever they thought they needed at the time. This was particularly true of those inmates who had been hooked on drugs prior to being incarcerated.

There is a theory that has been recently developed stating that a person who became addicted to mind-altering substance would sometime cease to continue to develop emotionally or mentally even as a person who was not addicted to substances. In my own way, I set out to test this theory and was amazed at the thirty or forty-something years old person who acted as if they were in their teens and early twenties. When I asked, politely of course, when they started using drugs, the age they gave me pretty much matched up to what the theory states. In other words, their development halted when the drugs took over.

I am by no means a specialist or psychiatrist, but this foray of mine into the mind of addicted individuals turned the light on for me in this area. Plus, it sometimes explained why a forty-year-old male had the same attitudes and actions of a teenager, with all the eye rolling and temper tantrums that sometimes go with it.

This takes us back to the respect part of this book. Now I'm not laying blame on anyone's doorstep for these poor often misguided souls, but one has to wonder if they were ever taught to respect themselves. Were they ever taught right from wrong from others who were responsible for it?

Maybe the person who was the teacher didn't know how to talk to children as we have gone over in this work. Maybe they too were from a dysfunctional family and often that is the problem. They repeat the same mistakes that their parents did, and their parents before them. Who knows?

Plus, today, we see so much violence being reported in schools today. Is this the only way kids, as far away from graduation as the middle school years, to seek attention? What has gone so horribly wrong that kids literally kill each over seemingly simple thing? Or is it something as simple as respect for other's opinions or empathy for what people are going through.

This book has been divided into three distinct sections. First of all, we started out with respect. Secondly, we looked at how to get children to really listen, and lastly, we discussed how to get them to learn.

Getting kids to listen can sometimes turn into a battle. Especially in those teen years when the hormones start raging and they are developmentally at the point they are trying to pull away so they can make their own way out in the big world.

It is especially important at this stage that the parents keep their heads and wits about them. It is especially important to use some of the techniques we discussed on how to not compare one child to another or belittle or nag or even make them feel stupid and inadequate.

Many times, parents don't even realize they are doing this. After all, life today is hectic. Parents work and have so many other things to do, it is difficult to come home and confront all the problems their children have brought home with them from school. But, is important that we do.

Perhaps if we do, we can prevent these children from doing harm to themselves or others. Perhaps we can make a child feel good about themselves and their abilities and they will not feel as if they have to turn to drugs or alcohol or any other activity to make them feel whole and valued again.

I hope you will allow me to take you back with me to my early childhood. I was the oldest of three. I was also a stepchild, which put me in a precarious situation. I can honestly say I never felt really young, for people depended on me to take care of my younger siblings and the house while my mom and stepfather worked.

I wasn't allowed to participate in after-school activities since I was needed at home to take care of the others. I was often called dorky, a nerd, and some other words I will not include here. There were times too when I was told I would never 'amount to anything'.

I remember the last time I was told this. I remember it well. I also remember that I made up my mind then and there that I would show all those people who did not believe that I could make anything of myself that they were wrong.

Thankfully, my mental attitude was strong enough to withstand the insensitive and often malicious things I was told. Today, I hold four degrees and am currently working toward a doctorate. So, there!

I was blessed enough to have teachers in high school who turned into role models for me. Looking back, they supported my attempts at becoming more than most people thought I could be. They used many of the techniques included in this work. So, I am a living testament that these ideas regarding how to talk to kids so they will learn respect, so they will listen, and so they will learn do work.

I hope you have enjoyed this work. I have shared some of the things that I have learned over the years. I have cited theories that in my own humble way, I have tested and found to be at least partially true. It is my goal that by reading these words, you and I together can help our children be at the top of their game. To become good citizens of not only our country but also the world. To make it a better place.

Questions to Ponder:

1. Take an in-depth and honest look at you and your child's relationship. What perspective or habits do you see? What would you like to change?

Current Habit	*New Habit*
a)	*a)*
b)	*b)*
c)	*c)*

2. What are the reasons for current dissatisfaction with the relationship and what steps have you previously tried to change the interaction and relationship?

   Reasons:

   a.

   b.

   c.

   Steps:

   a.

   b.

   c.

3. Did the Above steps successfully change the behavior or improve your relationship? If not, reassess the problem below, and try to pinpoint the cause.

95

a.

b.

c.

4. How did you deal with the unacceptable behavior in the past and what you plan to do now that you have read this book?

What You did before	*What You will do Now*
a)	a)
b)	b)
c)	c)

5. What suggestions have you followed from other works? Did they help?

   a.

   b.

   c.

   d.

   e.

6. What buttons does your child push to make you upset?

   a.

   b.

   c.

   d.

e.

f.

7. What are the techniques you usually follow when an unacceptable behavior occurs with your child?

   a.

   b.

   c.

8. What you have noticed pushes your child's buttons that can lead to unacceptable behavior, such as acting out, or other behaviors?

   a.

   b.

   c.

9. Which mistakes do you make regularly, such as yelling or criticizing?

    a.

    b.

    c.

    d.

10. What do you do for quiet time before addressing the problems of the day? What quiet times do you employ with your child?

    a.

    b.

    c.

d.

11. How can you encourage self-discipline in your child?

a.

b.

c.

d.

12. Do you take your child's actions personally? What will you do to change this feeling?

a.

b.

c.

13. A six-month plan to change attitudes and actions. (yes, it can take longer, but this is a start.)

   Today:

   1 month:

   3 months:

   6 months:

Feeling after noticing less frustration and confrontations:

✓

✓

✓

✓

✓

✓

✓

✓

✓

14. What changes do you want in your life after reading this
    book?

Incident	How you would have reacted before	How you will react now.
➤ ➤ ➤ ➤ ➤		
➤ ➤ ➤ ➤ ➤		

15. What other actions can you think off that will help to improve you and your child's behavior and interactions? Please include age-appropriate tasks and plans as the child ages.

    a.

    b.

    c.

    d.

    e.

THE END

CPSIA information can be obtained
at www.ICGtesting.com
Printed in the USA
LVHW081508290920
667401LV00004B/1274